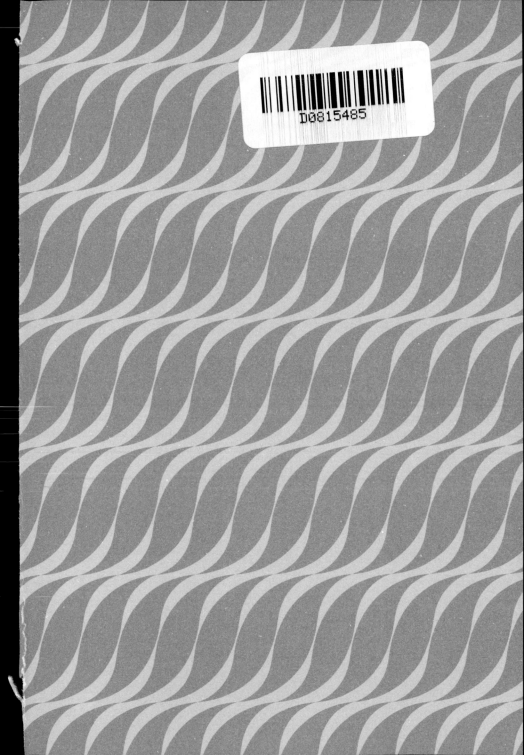

QUICK & EASY
PIZZAS

Consulting Editor:
Valerie Ferguson

southwater

Contents

Introduction

The pizza is the world's favorite fast food—a crisp, golden crust topped with melted cheese, tomatoes and almost any other savory ingredient from artichokes to ham, smoked salmon to spinach. It originated in Naples as a simple and inexpensive snack that was easy to eat with the fingers and has never looked back since leaving its native city.

This book includes recipes for basic dough, a super-fast version for those in a hurry and a fail-safe method with a food processor. Nowadays, too, it is possible to buy fresh, frozen or long-life pizza crusts at most supermarkets. Although they never taste quite as good as the homemade variety, they can be very useful to have on hand.

As for toppings—the choice is virtually limitless. You can include or omit almost anything you like—from pepperoni to cheese. The recipes in this book range from classics to hearty meaty versions, from fish and shellfish-topped options and to vegetarian concoctions. As well as being a convenient snack, pizza, perhaps served with a salad, is a filling lunch or supper. Little pizzettes and thin wedges of pizza also make stylish appetizers and wonderful party food.

Ingredients

A range of fresh and staple ingredients and a selection of herbs and spices will enable you to make pizzas with flair and flavor.

Olive Oil: Used for making the crust, brushing, pre-cooking toppings and for drizzling on the finished pizza. A good olive oil is essential. It may be flavored with herbs and spices.

Herbs & Spices: Fresh herbs are best. Basil has an affinity with tomatoes. Parsley and thyme are "all-purpose" herbs, and chives give a hint of onion. Oregano features widely in Italian cuisine. Sage, which has a strong flavor, is also used.

Chiles are essential for hot and spicy pizzas. Salt and black pepper bring out the full flavor of other ingredients. Other useful spices include ground cumin and grated nutmeg.

Cheeses: Mozzarella, with its stretchy melting quality, is a popular choice for pizzas. Ricotta is used for its mild flavor, and Gruyère, dolcelatte, feta, goat cheese, Pecorino and Parmesan provide flavors that contrast well with fresh vegetables.

Fish & Shellfish:
Shrimp, mussels, squid and salmon are delicious toppings. Canned fish, such as tuna and anchovies, are traditional and very convenient.

Shrimp

Poultry & Fresh Meat: Chicken —both fresh and smoked—is versatile. Lean ground beef cooks quickly and is easy to arrange evenly on pizza.

Cured Meats: Traditional toppings include spicy sausages, such as pepperoni, prosciutto and other kinds of ham, and a range of sliced meats. Most of these are available at larger supermarkets.

Vegetables: Used on their own or with meat or fish, fresh vegetables are essential. Cultivated and wild mushrooms make wonderful toppings. Tomatoes, sliced or made into a sauce, are indispensable. Bell Peppers add color and flavor.

Bell Peppers

Staple Ingredients: Olives and capers are traditional toppings and add piquancy. Sun-dried tomatoes have a concentrated flavor, and the oil may also be used for cooking. Tomato paste and sun-dried tomato paste enrich sauces and toppings. Tapenade, a French olive paste, and pesto, an Italian herb sauce, may be used in the same way. Pine nuts add texture and extra flavor.

Olives

Basic Recipes

Basic Pizza Dough

This simple dough is rolled out thinly for a traditional pizza recipe.

Makes
1 10–12-inch round pizza crust
4 5-inch round pizza crusts
1 12 x 7-inch rectangular
pizza crust

INGREDIENTS
1½ cups all-purpose flour
¼ teaspoon salt
1 teaspoon active dry yeast
½–⅔ cup lukewarm water
1 tablespoon olive oil

2 Knead the dough on a lightly floured surface for about 10 minutes, until smooth and elastic.

3 Place the dough in a greased bowl, and cover with plastic wrap. Let sit in a warm place to rise for about 1 hour or until the dough has doubled in size.

4 Punch down the dough. Turn onto a lightly floured surface, and knead again for 2–3 minutes. Roll out as needed and place on a greased baking sheet. Push up the dough to make a rim. The dough is now ready for your choice of topping.

1 Sift the flour and salt into a large mixing bowl. Stir in the yeast. Make a well in the center of the dry ingredients. Pour in the water and oil and mix with a spoon into a soft dough.

Using a Food Processor

For speed, make the pizza dough in a food processor.

1 Put the flour, salt and yeast into a food processor. Process to mix. Measure the water and add the oil. With the machine running, add the liquid and process until the dough forms a soft ball. Let rest for 2 minutes, then process for 1 more minute.

2 Remove the dough from the processor and shape into a neat round. Place in a greased bowl and cover with plastic wrap. Let sit in a warm place for about 1 hour, until doubled in size. Punch down and knead the dough for 2–3 minutes. The dough is now ready to use.

Superquick Pizza Dough

If you're really pressed for time, try a packaged pizza dough mix.

Makes
1 10–12-inch round
pizza crust
4 5-inch round pizza crusts
1 12 x 7-inch rectangular
pizza crust

INGREDIENTS
5-ounce package pizza
    dough mix
½ cup lukewarm water

1 Empty the contents of the package into a mixing bowl. Pour in the water and mix with a wooden spoon into a soft dough.

2 Turn the dough onto a lightly floured surface and knead for 5 minutes, until smooth and elastic. The dough is now ready to use.

Tomato Sauce

Many of the recipes use tomato sauce as the basis of the topping on pizzas.

Covers
1 10–12-inch round
pizza crust
1 12 x 7-inch rectangular
pizza crust

INGREDIENTS
1 tablespoon olive oil
1 onion, finely chopped
1 garlic clove, crushed
14-ounce can chopped tomatoes
1 tablespoon tomato paste
1 tablespoon chopped fresh mixed herbs,
    such as parsley, thyme, basil and oregano
pinch of sugar
salt and freshly ground black pepper

1 Heat the oil in a pan and sauté the onion and garlic until softened. Add the tomatoes, tomato paste, herbs, sugar and seasoning.

2 Simmer, stirring occasionally, for about 45 minutes or until the tomatoes have reduced to a thick pulp.

Flavored Oils

For extra flavor brush these on the pizza crust before adding the topping. They also form a kind of protective seal that keeps the crust crisp and dry.

Chili

INGREDIENTS
⅔ cup olive oil
2 teaspoons tomato paste
1 tablespoon dried red chile flakes

1 Heat the oil in a pan until very hot but not smoking. Stir in the tomato paste and red chile flakes. Let cool. Pour the chili oil into a small jar or bottle. Cover and store in the refrigerator for up to 2 months.

Garlic

INGREDIENTS
3–4 garlic cloves
½ cup olive oil

1 Peel the garlic cloves and put them in a jar or bottle. Pour in the oil, cover and refrigerate for up to 1 month.

Margherita Pizza

This classic pizza is simple to prepare. The sweet flavor of sun-ripened tomatoes works wonderfully with the basil and mozzarella.

Serves 2–3

INGREDIENTS
1 pizza crust,
   10–12 inches in diameter
2 tablespoons olive oil
1 batch Tomato Sauce
5 ounces mozzarella cheese
2 ripe tomatoes, thinly sliced
6–8 fresh basil leaves
2 tablespoons freshly grated
   Parmesan cheese
freshly ground black pepper

2 With a sharp knife, cut the mozzarella into thin slices.

1 Preheat the oven to 425°F. Brush the pizza crust with 1 tablespoon of the oil and then spread on the tomato sauce.

COOK'S TIP: If available, try to use real Italian buffalo mozzarella cheese. The flavor is much better than other types.

3 Arrange the sliced mozzarella and tomatoes on top of the pizza crust in overlapping circles.

VARIATIONS: As with many tomato-based toppings, anchovies and/or capers can make an interesting addition.

You could also add a variety of thinly sliced vegetables, such as zucchini, slices of ham or sausage, nuts or flaked tuna, to this basic pizza before adding the cheese.

4 Roughly tear the basil leaves, and sprinkle them on the pizza. Sprinkle with the Parmesan. Drizzle on the remaining oil and season with black pepper. Bake for 15–20 minutes, until crisp and golden. Serve immediately.

Marinara Pizza

The combination of garlic, good quality olive oil and oregano give this pizza an unmistakably Italian flavor.

Serves 2–3

INGREDIENTS
¼ cup olive oil
1½ pounds plum tomatoes, peeled,
    seeded and chopped
1 pizza crust,
    10–12 inches in diameter
4 garlic cloves, cut into slivers
1 tablespoon chopped
    fresh oregano
salt and freshly ground
    black pepper

1 Preheat the oven to 425°F. Heat 2 tablespoons of the oil in a pan. Add the tomatoes and cook, stirring frequently, for about 5 minutes, until soft.

2 Place the tomatoes in a sieve and let drain for about 5 minutes.

3 Transfer the tomatoes to a food processor or blender and process into a smooth purée.

4 Brush the pizza crust with half the remaining oil. Spoon on the tomatoes and sprinkle with garlic and oregano. Drizzle on the remaining oil and season with salt and pepper. Bake for 15–20 minutes, until crisp and golden. Serve immediately.

VARIATION: The garlic flavor can be made milder by blanching the whole cloves in boiling water for 2 minutes before slicing.

Quattro Formaggi Pizza

Topped with four cheeses, these individual pizzas are quick to assemble, and the aroma, while they are cooking, is irresistible. They make a delicious light lunch, served with a crisp green salad.

Serves 4

INGREDIENTS
5-inch round
    pizza crusts
1 tablespoon Garlic Oil
½ small red onion, very
    thinly sliced
2 ounces dolcelatte cheese
2 ounces mozzarella cheese
½ cup grated
    Gruyère cheese
2 tablespoons freshly grated
    Parmesan cheese
1 tablespoon chopped
    fresh thyme
freshly ground black pepper

2 Cut the dolcelatte and mozzarella into cubes and sprinkle on the crusts.

3 Combine the Gruyère, Parmesan and thyme and sprinkle on top.

VARIATION: An aged Farmhouse Cheddar is a good substitute if Gruyère cheese is not available.

1 Preheat the oven to 425°F. Place the pizza crusts well apart on two greased baking sheets, then push up the dough edges to make a thin rim. Brush with garlic oil and top with the red onion.

14

4 Grind on plenty of black pepper. Bake for 15–20 minutes, until crisp and golden and the cheese is bubbling. Serve immediately.

Fiorentina Pizza

Spinach is the star ingredient of this pizza. A grating of nutmeg to heighten its flavor gives this pizza its unique character.

Serves 2–3

INGREDIENTS
6 ounces spinach
3 tablespoons olive oil
1 small red onion, thinly sliced
1 pizza crust,
    10–12 inches in diameter
1 batch Tomato Sauce
freshly grated nutmeg
5 ounces mozzarella cheese
1 egg
¼ cup grated
    Gruyère cheese

1 Preheat the oven to 425°F. Remove and discard the spinach stems and wash the leaves in plenty of cold water. Drain well and pat dry with paper towels.

2 Heat 1 tablespoon of the olive oil and sauté the sliced red onion for about 5 minutes, until soft. Add the spinach and continue to cook until just wilted. Drain off any excess liquid.

3 Brush the pizza crust with half the remaining oil. Spread on the tomato sauce, then top with the spinach mixture. Grate on some nutmeg.

4 Thinly slice the mozzarella and arrange on the spinach. Drizzle on the remaining oil. Bake for 10 minutes, then remove from the oven.

VARIATION: Frozen spinach can be used, but be sure that it is properly thawed and thoroughly drained before using.

5 Make a small well in the center and drop the egg into the hole.

6 Sprinkle on the grated Gruyère cheese and return to the oven for another 5–10 minutes, until crisp and golden. Serve immediately.

Quattro Stagioni Pizza

The topping on this pizza is divided into four quarters, one for each season of the year. You may substitute any other seasonal favorites.

Serves 4

INGREDIENTS

1 pound peeled plum tomatoes,
   fresh or canned, weighed whole,
   without extra juice
5 tablespoons olive oil
1½ cups thinly
   sliced mushrooms
1 garlic clove, finely chopped
4 pizza crusts, 8 inches in diameter
3 cups mozzarella cheese,
   cut into small dice
4 thin slices of cooked ham, cut into
   2-inch squares
32 black olives, pitted and halved
8 artichoke hearts preserved in oil,
   drained and cut in half
1 teaspoon fresh oregano leaves
salt and freshly ground
   black pepper

1 Preheat the oven to 425°F. Strain the tomatoes through the medium holes of a food mill placed over a bowl, scraping in all the pulp.

2 Heat 2 tablespoons of the oil and lightly sauté the mushrooms. Stir in the garlic and set aside.

3 Spread the puréed tomato on the prepared pizza dough, leaving the rim uncovered. Sprinkle evenly with the mozzarella. Spread mushrooms on one quarter of the pizza.

4 Arrange the ham on another quarter, and the olives and artichoke hearts on the two remaining quarters. Sprinkle with oregano and the remaining olive oil and season to taste. Bake for 15–20 minutes or until the crust is golden brown.

Salmon & Avocado Pizza

Smoked and fresh salmon, mixed with avocado, make a delicious topping.
Try using smoked salmon trimmings, which are cheaper than slices.

Serves 3–4

INGREDIENTS

5 ounces salmon fillet
½ cup dry white wine
1 pizza crust, 10–12 inches in diameter
1 tablespoon olive oil
14-ounce can chopped tomatoes, drained well
1 cup grated mozzarella cheese
1 small avocado
2 teaspoons lemon juice
2 tablespoons crème fraîche
3 ounces smoked salmon, cut into strips
1 tablespoon capers, drained
2 tablespoons snipped fresh chives,
    to garnish
freshly ground black pepper

1 Preheat the oven to 425°F. Place
the salmon fillet in a frying pan, pour
in the wine and season with pepper.
Bring to a boil over low heat, remove
from heat, cover and cool. (The fish
will continue to cook.) Skin and flake
the salmon into small pieces, removing
any bones.

2 Brush the pizza crust with the oil
and spread on the drained tomatoes.
Sprinkle on ½ cup of the mozzarella.
Bake for 10 minutes, then remove
from the oven.

3 Meanwhile, halve, pit and peel the
avocado. Cut the flesh into small cubes
and toss in the lemon juice.

4 Dot teaspoons of the crème fraîche
on the pizza crust.

5 Arrange the fresh and smoked salmon, avocado, capers and remaining grated mozzarella on top. Season with freshly ground black pepper. Bake for another 5–10 minutes, until crisp and golden.

6 Sprinkle on the chives to garnish and serve the pizza immediately.

Tuna, Anchovy & Caper Pizza

This pizza makes a substantial supper dish, which will provide two to three generous portions when accompanied by a simple salad.

Serves 2–3

INGREDIENTS
2 tablespoons olive oil
1 batch Tomato Sauce
1 small red onion
7-ounce can tuna in water, drained
1 tablespoon capers, drained
12 pitted black olives
3 tablespoons freshly grated
    Parmesan cheese
2-ounce can anchovy fillets, drained
    and halved lengthwise
freshly ground black pepper

FOR THE SCONE PIZZA DOUGH
1 cup self-rising flour
1 cup self-rising
    whole-wheat flour
pinch of salt
¼ cup butter, diced
about ⅔ cup milk

1 Combine the flours and salt in a bowl. Add the diced butter and rub in until the mixture resembles fine bread crumbs. Add the milk and mix into a soft dough with a wooden spoon. Turn out onto a lightly floured surface and knead lightly until smooth.

2 Preheat the oven to 425°F. Roll out the dough on a lightly floured surface to a 10-inch circle. Place on a greased baking sheet and brush with 1 tablespoon of the oil. Spread the tomato sauce evenly on the dough.

3 Cut the onion into thin wedges and arrange on top. Roughly flake the drained tuna with a fork and sprinkle on the onion.

4 Sprinkle on the capers, black olives and Parmesan. Lattice the anchovy fillets to make a pattern on top of the pizza.

5 Drizzle on the remaining oil, then grind on plenty of black pepper. Bake for 5–10 minutes, until crisp and golden. Serve immediately.

Anchovy, Bell Pepper & Tomato Pizza

This pretty, summery pizza is utterly simple, yet quite delicious. It's well worth broiling the peppers, as they take on a delicious smoky flavor.

Serves 2–3

INGREDIENTS
6 plum tomatoes
3 tablespoons olive oil
1 teaspoon salt
1 large red bell pepper
1 large yellow bell pepper
1 pizza crust, 10–12 inches in diameter
2 garlic cloves, chopped
2-ounce can anchovy
    fillets, drained
freshly ground black pepper
fresh basil leaves,
    to garnish

2 Meanwhile, preheat the oven to 425°F. Slice the peppers in half lengthwise and remove the seeds. Place the pepper halves, skin-side up, on a baking sheet and broil until the skins are evenly charred.

1 Halve the tomatoes lengthwise and scoop out the seeds with a small spoon. Roughly chop the flesh and place in a bowl with 1 tablespoon of the oil and the salt. Mix well, then let marinate for 30 minutes.

3 Place the peppers in a covered bowl for 10 minutes, then peel off the skins. Cut the flesh into thin strips.

4 Brush the pizza crust with half the remaining oil. Drain the tomatoes, then sprinkle on the crust with the peppers and garlic.

5 Snip on the anchovy fillets and season with pepper. Drizzle on the remaining oil and bake for 15–20 minutes, until the crust is crisp and golden. Garnish with basil leaves and serve immediately.

Shellfish Pizza

Almost any combination of your favorite shellfish can be used as a pizza topping.

Serves 3–4

INGREDIENTS

1 pound peeled plum tomatoes,
   fresh or canned, weighed whole,
   without extra juice
6 ounces small squid
8 ounces fresh mussels
1 pizza crust, 10–12 inches in diameter
6 ounces shrimp, raw or cooked, peeled
   and deveined
2 garlic cloves, finely chopped
3 tablespoons chopped fresh parsley
salt and freshly ground black pepper
3 tablespoons olive oil

1 Preheat the oven to 425°F. Strain the tomatoes through the medium holes of a food mill placed over a bowl, scraping in all the pulp.

2 Clean the squid by first peeling off the thin skin from the body. Rinse well. Pull the head and tentacles off the sac. Some of the intestines will come off with the head.

3 Remove and discard the quill and any remaining insides from the sac. Sever the tentacles from the head. Discard the head and intestines. Remove the small hard beak from the base of the tentacles. Rinse the sac and tentacles under running water. Drain. Slice the sacs into thin rings ¼-inch thick.

4 Scrape the beard and any barnacles off the mussels and scrub well. Rinse in cold water. Discard any that are open or have broken shells. Place the mussels in a saucepan and heat until they open. Lift them out with a slotted spoon, and remove to a side dish. Discard any that do not open. Break off the empty half shells and discard.

5 Spread some of the puréed tomatoes on the pizza crust, leaving the rim uncovered. Dot evenly with the shrimp and squid rings and tentacles. Sprinkle with the garlic, parsley, salt and pepper, and olive oil.

6 Bake for about 8 minutes. Remove from the oven, and add the mussels in the half shells. Return to the oven and bake for 7–10 more minutes, until the crust is golden. Serve the pizza immediately.

Mussel & Leek Pizzettes

Serve these tasty pizzettes with a crisp green or mixed salad for
a light summer lunch.

Serves 4

INGREDIENTS
1 pound fresh mussels
½ cup dry white wine
5-inch round pizza crusts
1 tablespoon olive oil
2 ounces Gruyère cheese
2 ounces mozzarella cheese
2 small leeks
salt and freshly ground
    black pepper

1 Preheat the oven to 425°F. Place
the mussels in a bowl of cold water to
soak, and scrub well. Remove the
beards, scrape off any barnacles and
discard any mussels that are open or
have broken shells.

VARIATION: Frozen or canned
mussels can also be used, but will
not have the same flavor and
texture. Make sure you defrost the
mussels properly.

2 Place the mussels in a pan. Pour in
the wine, bring to a boil, cover and
cook over high heat, shaking the pan
occasionally, for 5–10 minutes, until
the mussels have opened.

3 Drain off the cooking liquid.
Remove the mussels from their shells,
discarding any that remain closed.
Let cool.

4 Place the pizza crusts well apart on
two greased baking sheets, then push
up the dough edges to form a thin
rim. Brush the pizza crusts with the
oil. Grate the cheeses and sprinkle half
evenly on the crusts.

5 Thinly slice the leeks, then sprinkle on the cheese. Bake for 10 minutes, then remove from the oven.

6 Arrange the mussels on top. Season and sprinkle on the remaining cheese. Bake for another 5–10 minutes, until crisp and golden and the cheese is bubbling. Serve immediately.

Shrimp & Sun-dried Tomato Pizzettes

Sun-dried tomatoes make an excellent topping for pizzas.

Serves 4

INGREDIENTS
1 batch Basic or Superquick Pizza Dough
2 tablespoons Chili Oil
¾ cup grated mozzarella cheese
1 garlic clove, chopped
½ small red onion, thinly sliced
4–6 pieces sun-dried tomatoes,
   thinly sliced
4 ounces cooked shrimp, peeled
2 tablespoons chopped fresh basil
salt and freshly ground black pepper
shredded fresh basil leaves, to garnish

1 Preheat the oven to 425°F. Divide the dough into eight equal pieces.

2 Roll out each one on a lightly floured surface to a small oval about ¼ inch thick. Place well apart on two greased baking sheets. Prick all over with a fork.

3 Brush the pizza crusts with 1 tablespoon of the chili oil and top with the grated mozzarella cheese, leaving a ½-inch border.

4 Divide the garlic, onion, sun-dried tomatoes, shrimp and basil among the pizza crusts. Season and drizzle on the remaining chili oil. Bake for 8–10 minutes, until crisp and golden. Garnish with shredded basil leaves and serve immediately.

Crab & Parmesan Calzonelli

If preferred, you can use shrimp instead of crab in these miniature calzone.

Makes 10–12

INGREDIENTS
1 batch Basic or Superquick Pizza Dough
4 ounces mixed prepared crabmeat,
    thawed if frozen
1 tablespoon heavy cream
2 tablespoons freshly grated
    Parmesan cheese
2 tablespoons chopped fresh parsley
1 garlic clove, crushed
salt and freshly ground black pepper
fresh parsley sprigs, to garnish

1 Preheat the oven to 400°F. Roll out the dough on a lightly floured surface to ⅛ inch thick. Using a 3-inch plain round cutter, stamp out 10–12 circles.

2 In a bowl combine the crabmeat, heavy cream, grated Parmesan, chopped fresh parsley, crushed garlic, salt and freshly ground black pepper.

3 Spoon a little of the filling on one half of each circle. Dampen the edges with water and fold over to completely enclose the filling.

4 Seal the edges by pressing with a fork. Place well apart on two greased baking sheets. Bake for 10–15 minutes, until golden brown and crisp. Garnish with parsley sprigs and serve immediately.

Chicken, Shiitake Mushroom & Cilantro Pizza

The addition of shiitake mushrooms adds an earthy flavor to this colorful pizza, while fresh red chile adds a hint of spiciness.

Serves 3–4

INGREDIENTS
3 tablespoons olive oil
12 ounces chicken breast fillets, skinned and
    cut into thin strips
1 bunch scallions, sliced
1 fresh red chile, seeded and chopped
1 red bell pepper, seeded and cut into thin strips
3 ounces fresh shiitake mushrooms, sliced
3–4 tablespoons chopped cilantro
1 pizza crust, 10–12 inches in diameter
1 tablespoon Chili Oil
5 ounces mozzarella cheese
salt and freshly ground black pepper

1 Preheat the oven to 425°F. Heat 2 tablespoons of the olive oil in a wok or large frying pan.

2 Add the chicken, scallions, chile, pepper and mushrooms and stir-fry over a high heat for 2–3 minutes. Do not overcook.

3 Season to taste with salt and pepper. Pour off any excess oil, then set aside the chicken mixture to cool. Stir the cilantro into the chicken mixture.

4 Brush the pizza crust with the chili oil. Spread on the chicken mixture and drizzle on the remaining olive oil.

COOK'S TIP: For the chicken mixture, cook the meat until firm but slightly pink inside or it will overcook in the oven.

5 Grate the mozzarella and sprinkle on. Bake for 15–20 minutes, until crisp and golden and the topping is bubbling. Serve immediately.

Hot and Spicy Pizza

This fiery pizza is spiced with green chiles, and the topping includes slices of pepperoni.

Serves 2–3

INGREDIENTS
1 pizza crust, 10–12 inches in diameter
1 tablespoon olive oil
4-ounce can peeled and chopped green chiles
   in brine, drained
1 batch Tomato Sauce
3 ounces sliced pepperoni
6 black olives
1 tablespoon chopped
   fresh oregano
1 cup grated
   mozzarella cheese
fresh oregano leaves,
   to garnish

1 Preheat the oven to 425°F. Brush the pizza crust with the olive oil.

2 Stir the green chiles into the tomato sauce, and spread the mixture evenly on the pizza crust.

3 Sprinkle the pepperoni slices on the tomato sauce and chili mixture.

4 Halve the olives lengthwise, and remove and discard the pit. Sprinkle the olive halves on the pepperoni, with the chopped oregano.

VARIATION: You can make this pizza as hot as you want. For a really fiery version, use fresh red or green chiles, seeded and cut into slices, instead of the chiles in brine. You could also substitute chorizo, which is even spicier, for the pepperoni.

5 Sprinkle on the grated mozzarella and bake for 15–20 minutes, until the pizza is crisp and golden.

6 Garnish with fresh oregano leaves and serve immediately.

Caramelized Onion, Salami & Black Olive Pizza

The sweetness of the caramelized onion is offset by the salty olives and herbs in the pizza crust and the sprinkling of Parmesan to finish.

Serves 4

INGREDIENTS
1½ pounds red onions
¼ cup olive oil
12 black olives
1 batch Basic or Superquick
   Pizza Dough
1 teaspoon dried *herbes de Provence*
6–8 slices Italian salami, quartered
2–3 tablespoons freshly grated
   Parmesan cheese
freshly ground black pepper

1 Preheat the oven to 425°F. Thinly slice the onions.

2 Heat 2 tablespoons of the oil in a pan and add the onions. Cover and cook gently for 15–20 minutes, stirring occasionally, until the onions are soft and very lightly colored. Let cool.

3 Cut the olives in half lengthwise, remove and discard the pits. Finely chop the olives.

4 Knead the dough on a lightly floured surface, adding the black olives and *herbes de Provence*. Roll out the dough and use to line a 12 x 7-inch jelly roll pan. Push up the dough edges to make a thin rim and brush with half the remaining oil.

5 Spoon half the onions evenly on the crust, then top with the quartered salami slices and the remaining onions.

6 Grind on plenty of black pepper and drizzle on the remaining oil. Bake for 15–20 minutes, until crisp and golden. Remove from the oven and sprinkle on the freshly grated Parmesan to serve.

Pancetta, Leek & Smoked Mozzarella Pizza

Smoked mozzarella with its brownish smoky-flavored skin, pancetta and leeks make this an extremely tasty and easy-to-prepare pizza.

Serves 4

INGREDIENTS
2 tablespoons freshly grated
  Parmesan cheese
1 batch Basic or Superquick
  Pizza Dough
2 tablespoons olive oil
2 medium leeks, trimmed
8–12 slices pancetta
5 ounces smoked mozzarella cheese
freshly ground black pepper

1 Preheat the oven to 425°F. Dust the work surface with the Parmesan, then knead into the dough.

2 Divide the dough into four pieces and roll out each one to a 5-inch circle. Place well apart on two greased baking sheets, then push up the edges to make a thin rim. Brush the crusts with 1 tablespoon of the oil.

3 Thinly slice the leeks. Arrange the pancetta and leeks evenly on the four pizza crusts.

4 Grate the smoked mozzarella and sprinkle on top. Drizzle on the remaining oil and season with pepper. Bake for 15–20 minutes, until crisp and golden. Serve immediately.

Prosciutto, Mushroom & Artichoke Pizza

Here is a pizza full of rich and varied flavors. Use lots of different kinds of mushrooms.

Serves 2–3

INGREDIENTS
4 bottled artichoke hearts in oil, drained
4 tablespoons olive oil
1 bunch scallions, chopped
3¼ cups sliced mushrooms
2 garlic cloves, chopped
1 pizza crust, 10–12 inches in diameter
8 slices prosciutto
¼ cup freshly grated Parmesan cheese
salt and freshly ground black pepper
fresh thyme sprigs, to garnish

1 Preheat the oven to 425°F. Slice the artichokes.

2 Heat 2 tablespoons of the oil in a frying pan. Add the scallions, mushrooms and garlic and sauté over medium heat until all the juices have evaporated. Season with salt and pepper and let cool.

3 Brush the pizza crust with half the remaining oil. Arrange the prosciutto, mushrooms and artichoke hearts on top.

4 Sprinkle on the Parmesan, then drizzle on the remaining oil and season. Bake for 15–20 minutes. Garnish with thyme sprigs and serve immediately.

Calzone

A calzone is a pizza made from a round or a rectangular-shaped crust, folded over to enclose its filling. It can be eaten hot or cold.

Serves 4

INGREDIENTS
2 batches Basic Pizza Dough
1½ cups ricotta cheese
1 cup cooked ham, cut into
　　small dice
6 medium tomatoes, peeled, seeded
　　and diced
8 fresh basil leaves, torn into pieces
1½ cups mozzarella cheese,
　　cut into small dice
¼ cup freshly grated
　　Parmesan cheese
salt and freshly ground
　　black pepper
olive oil, for brushing

1 Preheat the oven to 475°F. Divide the dough into four balls. Roll each ball out into a flat circle about ¼ inch thick.

2 Combine all the remaining ingredients except the oil in a bowl, and mix well. Season to taste.

3 Divide the filling among the four circles of dough, placing it on half of each circle and allowing a border of ¾ inch all around.

4 Fold the other half of the circle over. Crimp the edges of the dough together with your fingers to seal.

COOK'S TIP: The calzone is a specialty of Naples. Calzone means "trouser leg" in Italian. This pizza was so named because it resembled a leg of the baggy trousers worn by Neapolitan men in the 18th and 19th centuries.

5 Brush the calzone tops lightly with olive oil. Place them on lightly oiled baking sheets. Bake for 15–20 minutes or until the tops are golden brown and the dough is puffed.

Chili Pizza

Ground beef, red kidney beans and smoky cheese combined with oregano, cumin and chiles give this pizza a Mexican character.

Serves 4

INGREDIENTS
2 tablespoons olive oil
1 red onion, finely chopped
1 garlic clove, crushed
½ red bell pepper, seeded and finely chopped
1½ cups lean ground beef
½ teaspoon ground cumin
2 fresh red chiles, seeded and chopped
4 ounces (drained weight) canned
   red kidney beans
1 batch Basic or Superquick Pizza Dough
1 batch Tomato Sauce
1 tablespoon chopped fresh oregano
½ cup grated mozzarella cheese
¾ cup grated smoked
   Cheddar cheese
salt and freshly ground black pepper

2 Add the cumin and chiles and continue to cook, stirring, for about 5 minutes. Add the beans and seasoning to taste.

3 Knead the dough on a lightly floured surface, roll out and use to line a 12 x 7-inch greased jelly roll pan. Push up the dough edges to make a rim.

1 Preheat the oven to 425°F. Heat 1 tablespoon of the oil in a frying pan. Add the onion, garlic and red pepper and gently sauté until soft. Increase the heat, add the beef and brown well, stirring constantly.

4 Spread the tomato sauce evenly on the pizza crust.

5 Spoon on the beef and beans mixture in an even layer, then sprinkle on the oregano.

6 Sprinkle on the cheeses and bake for 15–20 minutes, until crisp and golden. Serve immediately.

COOK'S TIP: This beef sauce, before the beans are added, can be prepared in advance and kept for up to 3 days in the refrigerator.

43

Spring Vegetable & Pine Nut Pizza

This colorful pizza is packed with delicious vegetables. You can vary the ingredients according to availability.

Serves 2–3

INGREDIENTS
1 pizza crust, 10–12 inches in diameter
3 tablespoons Garlic Oil
1 batch Tomato Sauce
4 scallions
2 zucchini
1 leek
4 ounces asparagus tips
1 tablespoon chopped fresh oregano
2 tablespoons pine nuts
½ cup grated mozzarella cheese
2 tablespoons freshly grated
    Parmesan cheese
freshly ground black pepper

1 Preheat the oven to 425°F. Brush the pizza crust with 1 tablespoon of the garlic oil, then spread on the tomato sauce.

2 Slice the scallions, zucchini, leek and asparagus tips.

3 Heat half the remaining garlic oil in a frying pan and stir-fry the vegetables for 3–5 minutes.

4 Arrange the vegetables in an even layer on the tomato sauce.

5 Sprinkle the chopped fresh oregano and the pine nuts on the pizza.

COOK'S TIP: Prepare scallions by first trimming off the outer skin. Then chop all the white and some of the green stems.

6 Combine the mozzarella and Parmesan and sprinkle on the pizza. Drizzle on the remaining garlic oil and season generously with pepper. Bake for 15–20 minutes, until crisp and golden. Serve immediately.

Mushroom & Pesto Pizza

This is a mouthwatering Mediterranean-style pizza.

Serves 4

INGREDIENTS
¾ cup fresh basil
¼ cup pine nuts
1½ ounces Parmesan cheese, thinly sliced
7 tablespoons olive oil
1 cup dried porcini mushrooms
2 onions, thinly sliced
3¼ cups chestnut
    mushrooms, sliced
1 pizza crust, 10–12 inches in diameter
salt and freshly ground black pepper

1 First, make the pesto topping. Place the basil, pine nuts, Parmesan and 5 tablespoons of the olive oil in a blender or food processor and process to make a smooth paste. Set aside.

2 Soak the dried mushrooms in hot water for 20 minutes.

3 Sauté the onions in the remaining olive oil for 3–4 minutes, until beginning to color. Add the chestnut mushrooms and cook for 2 minutes. Stir in the drained porcini mushrooms and season lightly.

4 Preheat the oven to 425°F. Lightly grease a large baking sheet and place the pizza crust on it.

5 Spread the pesto mixture to within ½ inch of the edge. Spread the mushroom mixture on top. Bake the pizza for 35–40 minutes, until risen and golden. Serve immediately.

Sicilian Pizza

This robust-flavored pizza is topped with roasted eggplant and cheese.

Serves 2

INGREDIENTS
1 small eggplant, cut into thin rounds
2 tablespoons olive oil
½ batch Basic or Superquick
    Pizza Dough
½ batch Tomato Sauce
6 ounces mozzarella cheese, sliced
½ cup pitted black olives
1 tablespoon capers, drained
¼ cup grated Pecorino cheese
salt and freshly ground black pepper

1 Preheat the oven to 400°F. Place the eggplant rounds on an oiled baking sheet and brush with the olive oil.

2 Bake for 10–15 minutes, turning once, until browned and tender. Remove the eggplant slices and drain on paper towels.

3 Increase the oven temperature to 425°F. Roll out the pizza dough to two 8-inch rounds. Transfer to baking sheets and spread on the tomato sauce.

4 Pile the eggplant slices on top of the tomato sauce and cover with the mozzarella. Dot with the black olives and capers. Sprinkle the Pecorino liberally on top, and season with plenty of salt and pepper. Bake for 15–20 minutes, until the crust on each pizza is golden. Serve immediately.

Zucchini, Corn & Plum Tomato Whole-Wheat Pizza

This tasty whole-wheat pizza can be served hot or cold with a mixed bean salad and fresh crusty bread or baked potatoes.

Serves 6

INGREDIENTS
2 cups whole-wheat flour
pinch of salt
2 teaspoons baking powder
¼ cup margarine
⅔ cup milk
2 tablespoons tomato purée
2 teaspoons dried *herbes de Provence*
2 teaspoons olive oil
1 onion, sliced
1 garlic clove, crushed
2 small zucchini, sliced
1½ cups sliced mushrooms
⅔ cup frozen
    corn kernels
2 plum tomatoes, sliced
½ cup finely grated
    Red Leicester cheese
½ cup finely grated
    mozzarella cheese
salt and freshly ground
    black pepper
fresh basil sprigs, to garnish

1 Preheat the oven to 425°F. Line a baking sheet with nonstick baking paper. Put the flour, salt and baking powder in a bowl and rub the margarine lightly into the flour until the mixture has the texture of fine bread crumbs.

2 Add enough milk, a little at a time, to form a soft dough and knead lightly. Roll the dough out on a lightly floured surface, to a circle about 10 inches in diameter.

3 Place the dough on the prepared baking sheet and make the edges slightly thicker than the center. Spread the tomato paste on the crust and sprinkle the dried herbs on top.

4 Heat the oil in a frying pan, add the onion, garlic, zucchini and mushrooms and cook gently for 10 minutes, stirring occasionally.

5 Spread the vegetable mixture on the pizza crust and sprinkle on the corn and seasoning. Arrange the tomato slices on top.

6 Combine the cheeses and sprinkle on the pizza. Bake for 25–30 minutes, until cooked and golden brown. Serve the pizza hot or cold in slices, garnished with basil sprigs.

COOK'S TIP: This pizza is ideal for freezing in slices. Freeze for up to 3 months.

Roasted Vegetable & Goat Cheese Pizza

Here is a pizza that incorporates the smoky flavors of oven-roasted vegetables with the distinctive taste of goat cheese.

Serves 3

INGREDIENTS
1 eggplant, cut into thick chunks
2 zucchini, halved and sliced lengthwise
1 red bell pepper, quartered and seeded
1 yellow bell pepper, quartered and seeded
1 small red onion, cut into wedges
6 tablespoons Garlic Oil
1 pizza crust, 10–12 inches in diameter
14-ounce can chopped tomatoes,
   drained well
4 ounces goat cheese (with rind)
1 tablespoon chopped fresh thyme
freshly ground black pepper
ready-made green olive tapenade, to serve

2 Remove the peppers from the oven and transfer to a plastic bag, using tongs. Seal the top and set aside. When they are cool enough to handle, peel off the skins and cut the flesh into thick strips.

3 Brush the pizza crust with half the remaining garlic oil and spread on the drained tomatoes.

1 Preheat the oven to 425°F Place the eggplant, zucchini, peppers and onion in a large roasting pan. Brush with 4 tablespoons of the garlic oil. Roast for about 30 minutes, turning the peppers and zucchini halfway through cooking.

4 Arrange the roasted vegetables evenly on top of the pizza crust.

5 Cut the goat cheese into chunks and arrange them on top of the vegetables. Sprinkle on the thyme.

6 Drizzle on the remaining garlic oil and season with pepper. Bake for 15–20 minutes, until crisp and golden. Spoon on the tapenade to serve.

New Potato & Garlic Pizza

A strongly-flavored pizza that makes the most of the new season's potatoes.

Serves 2–3

INGREDIENTS
12 ounces new potatoes
3 tablespoons olive oil
2 garlic cloves, crushed
1 pizza crust, 10–12 inches in diameter
1 red onion, thinly sliced
1¼ cups grated smoked mozzarella cheese
2 teaspoons chopped fresh rosemary
salt and freshly ground black pepper
2 tablespoons freshly grated Parmesan
    cheese, to garnish

1 Preheat the oven to 425°F. Cook the potatoes in boiling salted water for 5 minutes. Drain well. When cool, peel and slice thinly.

2 Heat 2 tablespoons of the oil in a frying pan. Add the sliced potatoes and garlic and cook for 5–8 minutes, until brown and tender.

3 Brush the pizza crust with the remaining oil. Sprinkle on the onion, then arrange the potatoes on top.

4 Sprinkle on the mozzarella and rosemary. Grind on plenty of pepper and bake for 15–20 minutes, until crisp and golden. Remove from the oven and sprinkle on the Parmesan to serve.

Butternut Squash & Sage

An unusual combination of sweet and savory ingredients.

Serves 4

INGREDIENTS
1 tablespoon butter
2 tablespoons olive oil
2 shallots, finely chopped
1 butternut squash, peeled, seeded and
   cubed, about 1 pound prepared weight
16 sage leaves
3 batches Basic or Superquick Pizza Dough
1½ batches Tomato Sauce
4 ounces sliced mozzarella cheese
½ cup firm goat cheese
salt and freshly ground black pepper

1 Preheat the oven to 400°F. Heat the butter and oil in a roasting pan and add the shallots, squash and half the sage leaves.

2 Toss the vegetables to coat and roast for 15–20 minutes, until tender.

3 Raise the oven temperature to 425°F. Divide the pizza dough into four equal pieces and roll out into 8-inch rounds. Oil two large baking sheets.

4 Place each round on a baking sheet and spread with tomato sauce. Spoon the squash and shallot mixture on top.

5 Cover with mozzarella and crumbled goat cheese. Garnish with sage leaves, season and bake for 15–20 minutes, until the cheese has melted and the crust on each pizza has turned golden.

Smoked Salmon Pizzettes

Sophisticated mini pizzas topped with smoked salmon, crème fraîche and lumpfish roe make an extra special party canapé.

Makes 10–12

INGREDIENTS
1 batch Basic or Superquick
   Pizza Dough
1 tablespoon snipped fresh chives
1 tablespoon olive oil
3–4 ounces smoked salmon,
   cut into strips
¼ cup crème fraîche
2 tablespoons black lumpfish roe
fresh chives, to garnish

1 Preheat the oven to 400°F. Knead the dough gently, adding the snipped chives until evenly mixed.

2 Roll out the dough on a lightly floured surface to about ⅛ inch thick. Using a 3-inch plain round cutter, stamp out 10–12 circles.

3 Place the crusts well apart on two greased baking sheets, prick all over with a fork, then brush with the oil. Bake for 10–15 minutes, until the crusts are crisp and golden.

4 Arrange the smoked salmon on top, then spoon on the crème fraîche. Spoon a tiny amount of lumpfish roe in the center and garnish with chives. Serve immediately.

Anchovy & Pesto Pizzettes

These delightful little pizzas combine the piquancy of olives and capers with anchovies and mozzarella cheese.

Makes 24

INGREDIENTS
2 batches Basic or Superquick
  Pizza Dough
¼ cup olive oil
2 tablespoons red pesto
12 pitted black olives
3 ounces mozzarella cheese, cubed
2 ounces (drained weight) sun-dried
  tomatoes in oil, chopped
2–3 tablespoons capers, drained
2-ounce can anchovy fillets, drained and
  roughly chopped
2 tablespoons freshly grated Parmesan
  cheese
fresh parsley sprigs, to garnish

1 Preheat the oven to 425°F.

2 Roll out the dough on a lightly floured surface to about ⅛ inch thick. Using a 2-inch plain round cutter, stamp out 24 rounds. Place the rounds on two greased baking sheets.

3 Brush the crusts with 2 tablespoons of the oil, then spread on the pesto.

4 Cut the olives into quarters lengthwise, then sprinkle the mozzarella, sun-dried tomatoes, capers and anchovies on the crusts.

5 Sprinkle on the Parmesan and drizzle on the remaining oil. Bake for 8–10 minutes, until crisp and golden. Transfer to a warm platter, garnish with parsley sprigs and serve.

Smoked Chicken, Yellow Bell Pepper and Sun-dried Tomato Pizzettes

These ingredients complement each other perfectly and make a really delicious and colorful topping.

Serves 4

INGREDIENTS
1 batch Basic or Superquick
    Pizza Dough
3 tablespoons olive oil
¼ cup sun-dried tomato paste
2 yellow bell peppers, seeded and cut
    into thin strips
6 ounces sliced smoked chicken or
    turkey, chopped
1¼ cups mozzarella
    cheese, cubed
2 tablespoons chopped fresh basil
salt and freshly ground
    black pepper

1 Preheat the oven to 425°F. Divide the prepared dough into four equal pieces and roll out each one on a lightly floured surface to a 5-inch circle.

2 Place well apart on two greased baking sheets, then push up the dough edges to make a thin rim. Brush with 1 tablespoon of the oil.

3 Brush the pizza crusts generously with the sun-dried tomato paste and set aside.

4 Stir-fry the peppers in half the remaining oil for 3–4 minutes.

5 Arrange the chicken and peppers on top of the sun-dried tomato paste.

VARIATION: For a vegetarian pizza with a similar smoky taste, omit the chicken, roast the yellow peppers and remove the skins before using, and replace the mozzarella with Bavarian smoked cheese.

6 Sprinkle over the mozzarella and basil. Season with salt and pepper.

7 Drizzle on the remaining oil and bake for 15–20 minutes, until crisp and golden. Serve immediately.

Spinach & Ricotta Panzerotti

These make great party food to serve with drinks or tasty appetizers for a crowd of hungry guests.

Makes 20–24

INGREDIENTS
4 ounces frozen chopped spinach,
   thawed and squeezed dry
¼ cup ricotta cheese
⅔ cup freshly
   grated Parmesan
generous pinch freshly
   grated nutmeg
2 batches Basic or Superquick
   Pizza Dough
1 egg white, lightly beaten
vegetable oil, for deep-frying
salt and freshly ground
   black pepper

1 Place the spinach, ricotta, Parmesan, nutmeg and seasoning in a bowl and beat until smooth.

COOK'S TIP: Do serve these as soon as possible after frying, as they will become much less appetizing if left to cool.

2 Roll out the dough on a lightly floured surface to about ⅛ inch thick. Using a 3-inch plain round cutter, stamp out 20–24 circles.

3 Spread a teaspoon of spinach mixture on one half of each circle.

4 Brush the edges of the dough with a little egg white.

5 Fold the dough over the filling and press the edges firmly together to seal.

6 Heat the oil in a large, heavy pan or deep-fat fryer to 350°F. Deep-fry the panzerotti, a few at a time, for 2–3 minutes, until golden. Drain thoroughly on paper towels and serve immediately.

Spicy Sun-dried Tomato Pizza Wedges

These spicy pizza wedges can be made with or without the pepperoni.

Makes 32

INGREDIENTS
3–4 tablespoons olive oil
2 onions, thinly sliced
2 garlic cloves, chopped
3¼ cups mushrooms, sliced
8 ounces canned chopped tomatoes
8 ounces pepperoni or cooked Italian-style
    spicy sausage, chopped
1 teaspoon chile flakes
1 teaspoon dried oregano
4 ounces sun-dried tomatoes, packed in oil,
    drained and sliced
1 pound bottled marinated artichoke hearts,
    well drained and cut into quarters
2 cups mozzarella cheese, grated
¼ cup freshly grated Parmesan cheese
pitted black olives, to garnish
fresh basil leaves, to garnish
strips of red bell pepper, to garnish
FOR THE DOUGH
cornmeal, for dusting
2 batches Basic or Superquick
    Pizza Dough
1 tablespoon virgin olive oil

1 In a large, deep frying pan, heat the oil over medium–high heat. Add the onions and cook for 3–5 minutes, until softened. Add the garlic and sliced mushrooms and cook for 3–4 more minutes, until the mushrooms begin to soften and color.

2 Stir in the chopped tomatoes, pepperoni or sausage, chile flakes and oregano and simmer for 20–30 minutes, stirring frequently, until thickened and reduced. Stir in the sun-dried tomatoes and set aside to cool.

3 Preheat the oven to 475°F. Line one large or two smaller baking sheets with aluminum foil, shiny-side up. Sprinkle generously with cornmeal. Cut the dough in half and roll out each half to a 12-inch round. Transfer to the baking sheet and brush the dough with 1 tablespoon oil.

4 Spread the tomato sauce evenly on the crusts to within ½ inch of the edge. Bake for 5 minutes on the lowest shelf of the oven.

VARIATION: You could use chorizo instead of the pepperoni in this hot and spicy pizza.

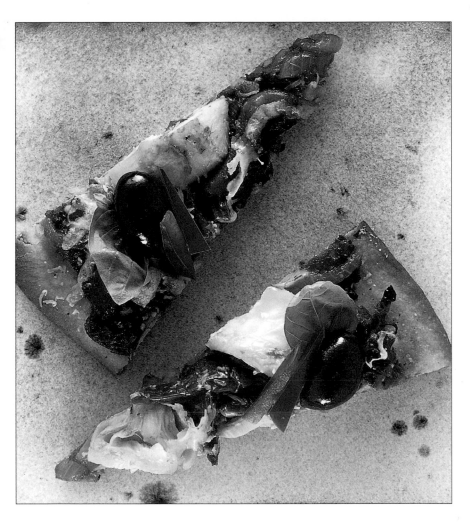

5 Arrange half the artichoke hearts on each crust, sprinkle evenly with the mozzarella and a little Parmesan. Drizzle with the remaining oil. Bake each one on the bottom shelf of the oven for 12–15 more minutes, until the edge of the crust is crisp and brown and the topping is golden and bubbling.

6 Remove to a wire rack to cool slightly. Slide the pizzas onto a cutting board and cut each into 16 thin wedges. Garnish each wedge with a black olive, a basil leaf and strips of red pepper, and serve as soon as possible.

61

Feta, Pimiento & Pine Nut Pizzettes

Delight your guests with these tempting small pizzas. Substitute goat cheese for the feta, if you prefer.

Makes 24

INGREDIENTS
2 batches Basic or Superquick
    Pizza Dough
all-purpose flour for rolling dough
4 tablespoons olive oil, plus extra for greasing
2 tablespoons ready-made black
    olive tapenade
6 ounces feta cheese
1 large canned pimiento, drained
2 tablespoons chopped fresh thyme
2 tablespoons pine nuts
freshly ground black pepper
fresh thyme sprigs, to garnish

2 Brush a thin layer of the black olive tapenade on each oval and crumble on the feta cheese.

3 Cut the pimiento into thin strips and pile evenly on top of the cheese.

1 Preheat the oven to 425°F. Divide the pizza dough into 24 pieces and roll out each one on a lightly floured surface to a small oval, about ⅛ inch thick. Place well apart on greased baking sheets and prick all over with a fork. Brush with 2 tablespoons of the oil.

4 Sprinkle each one with thyme and pine nuts. Drizzle on the remaining oil and grind on plenty of pepper. Bake for 10–15 minutes, until crisp and golden. Garnish with thyme sprigs and serve immediately.

This edition is published by Southwater

Distributed in the UK by
The Manning Partnership,
251–253 London Road East, Batheaston,
Bath BA1 7RL, UK
tel. (0044) 01225 852 727
fax. (0044) 01225 852 852

Distributed in Australia by
Sandstone Publishing,
Unit 1, 360 Norton Street, Leichhardt,
New South Wales 2040, Australia
tel. (0061) 2 9560 7888
fax. (0061) 2 9560 7488

Distributed in New Zealand by
Five Mile Press NZ,
PO Box 33–1071 Takapuna,
Auckland 9, New Zealand
tel. (0064) 9 4444 144
fax. (0064) 9 4444 518

Southwater is an imprint of Anness Publishing Limited

© 2000 Anness Publishing Limited

Publisher: Joanna Lorenz
Editor: Valerie Ferguson
Series Designer: Bobbie Colgate Stone
Designer: Andrew Heath
Production Controller: Joanna King

Recipes contributed by: Angela Boggiano,
Carla Capalbo, Jacqueline Clark, Shirley Gill,
Anne Sheasby, Elizabeth Wolf-Cohen,
Jeni Wright.

Photography: William Adams-Lingwood,
Karl Adamson, Joanna Farrow, Michelle Garrett, Amanda Heywood,
Janine Hosegood, David Jordan.

1 3 5 7 9 10 8 6 4 2